W9-CIR-416

Stranger Stop
and Cast an Eye

Stranger Stop
and Cast an Eye

. . . .

A GUIDE TO

GRAVESTONES &

GRAVESTONE RUBBING

G. Walker Jacobs

WITH PHOTOGRAPHS AND RUBBINGS

BY THE AUTHOR

THE STEPHEN GREENE PRESS

Brattleboro, Vermont

THIRD EDITION

This book has been produced
in the United States of America:
designed by R. L. Dothard Associates,
composed by American Book–Stratford Press, and printed
and bound by The Halliday Lithograph Corporation.
It is published by the Stephen Greene Press,
Brattleboro, Vermont 05301.
Library of Congress Catalog Card Number: 73–82745
International Standard Book Number: 0–8289–0189–9

73 74 75 76 77 78 79 9 8 7 6 5 4 3 2 1

For

JIM

CONTENTS

Stranger stop and cast an eye,

As you are now, so once was I,

As I am now, so you will be,

Prepare for death, and follow me.

INTRODUCTION

I HAVE divided *Stranger* into three chapters, the first historical, the second of a "how to" nature, and the third comprising examples of some of my own rubbings. I would suggest that your enjoyment of graveyard tours and stone rubbing will be enhanced by first reading the historical information, as this should enable you to appreciate the stones in their proper context. If you have a limited amount of time, you may want to go immediately to the set of instructions you are most interested in, leaving the historical section for leisurely reading later on.

Chapter 1, "A Brief History of Grave Symbols and Stonecutters," is only a sketch of the subject, and should be read as such. Broad generalizations are a necessary evil in a book of this length, and I hope that you will be aware that, in order to adequately cover any one of the topics mentioned, a full-length dissertation would be required. I have, at the end of the book, provided a list of books and articles (some of which I refer to in the text) that go into greater detail than I have been able to here; these are all very readable, written by reliable authorities, and are a must for anyone interested in serious study of American graveyard art.

Chapter 2, "Rubbing," provides a brief look at the Oriental beginnings of rubbing; its second section gets right into modern rubbing techniques. That section is written directly from my own experiences with the different rubbing methods. I hope that, with the aid of these instructions, rubbing will no longer be a figure-it-out-as-you-go hobby.

Chapter 3, "Some Rubbings by the Author," contains reproductions of a few of the rubbings I have done over the past years. All of the rubbings included were done using the dry method explained in Chapter 2.

With exception of those on pages 61, 62, 63, and 65, all illustrations in this book are by the author. Photographs of gravestones are identified by name, date, and geographic location, and, where possible, by the name of the burial ground.

When you go out to do rubbings, you should keep one thought in particular firmly in mind. If we hope not to have all American graveyards closed off to us (as has already happened with some), we must take as much care of them as possible. These burial grounds and gravestones have managed to survive the ravages of Time and Nature for over 250 years. With the increase in popular interest in them, and with so many people doing rubbings now, many of the graveyards are beginning to show the wear and tear that only Man seems able to inflict. It is important to remember to remove all tape and other refuse from the graveyards, and to be extremely careful when rubbing not to leave any traces of wax, ink, or whatever on the stone. If someone before you has been negligent, don't be too proud to clean up after him if you can. After all, you will only be hurting yourself in the long run if you don't.

If the graveyard is fenced off from the public, it is courteous to ask the caretaker for permission to enter.

Usually, with a cheerful smile and a brief explanation of what you intend to do, you can gain admittance, and often you will find yourself accompanied through the yard by a most knowledgeable and talkative companion.

Best wishes for sunny days and good rubbings!

Stranger Stop
and Cast an Eye

1. A Brief History of Grave
Symbols and Stonecutters

◄§ SYMBOLS AND THE EARLY
NEW ENGLANDER §►

SINCE ancient times it has been the practice to erect monuments or memorials to the dead, and the early New Englanders, in so many other ways iconoclastic, did not see fit to change this custom. Interestingly, it was only in their death rituals that the Puritans indulged in any sort of image-making, and it is in their graveyard art that we find an otherwise well-hidden, but deep-seated, naive belief in mystic symbolism. The gravestones of these deeply religious people were meant to teach the living as well as to commemorate the dead. In a world where images and symbols were forbidden in daily life, their gravestones must have enjoyed a much greater impact than they would in today's image-clogged society.

In order to understand the meaning of graveyard symbols, it is necessary first to understand a little of the basic psychology of symbolism. Let's divide all imagery into three classifications: *symbols, allegories,* and *signs.* While in practice it is not always easy to distinguish a symbol from an allegory or sign, theoretical definitions are helpful. A *symbol,* we will say, stands for the unknown, or for something greater than itself; an *allegory* changes the unknown into something known; and a *sign* stands for the known. We will not concern ourselves with allegories here, as they very rarely appear on New England's gravestones.

It is a generally accepted fact that people think in either denotative or connotative terms. In denotative terms, an image or picture refers specifically to the thing it describes—the picture of a heart in a biology textbook refers to a part of your body, nothing more or less. In connotative terms, an image suggests a meaning apart from the thing it explicitly names or describes—the picture of a heart on Valentine's Day suggests the warmth of love. According to our definitions, then, the picture of a heart in the biology book is a sign, whereas the Valentine's Day heart is a symbol. In this way we can see that the process of symbolization is one of projecting inner feelings (love) to external objects (the picture of a heart). It is this power to stand for something outside of, and greater than, itself that distinguishes a symbol from a mere sign.

When the New Englanders carved images on their stones, they were projecting their inner feelings about death and after-life onto the stones in the forms of symbols. Most often, stones were carved with a primary, or central, symbol, surrounded by secondary symbols. These secondary symbols were not meant to have specific meaning of their own, but rather were used to enhance the atmospheric feeling of the central symbol. For instance, we often find a death's-head as a central symbol, surrounded by an assortment of secondary mortality symbols such as hourglasses, scythes, or crossbones, all of which combine to give a fearsome reality to the feeling of Man's mortality (see Figure 1).

FIGURE 1: *Man is mortal, and his hour is brief: Winged hourglass and death's-head on the Edmund Mountfort stone, 1690. The Granary, Boston, Massachusetts.*

19

It should be understood that all symbols are totally culture-bound, and therefore must be studied within the context of the culture in which they appear. What is a symbol for one society may be only a sign for another, and vice versa. For instance, when we in the United States see someone driving down the street in a Cadillac bearing license number 1, we think, "Aha! There goes a man with both wealth and political power." To someone untutored in our way of life, the big fancy car with the low-number plates would be just that, a big fancy car with low-number plates. What was for us a symbol, standing for something outside itself, was to the foreigner a mere sign. We must be sure, then, as we study the graveyard art of the Puritans, that we have some understanding of their society and religion, or we shall misinterpret their symbols.

A PURITAN WORLD-VIEW

In the Puritan society of New England, men believed that in order to be able to distinguish between good and evil, one must be at all times rational, and yet on the other hand they felt that reason was too finite to comprehend God. Man, a reasoning creature, was not meant to have any immediate contact with his creator. The Puritans fully believed in the Calvinistic doctrine of predestination, and yet they considered it wrong not to work hard and accept responsibility in this world. Ideally working toward a kind of purification of their spirits, they prepared for salvation through the study of the Scriptures, and yet they believed that nothing they did in this world would assure them of salvation: only God could save. (Those who were saved—supposedly the members of the Puritan Church—were known as the "Elect.") The most predominant literary forms of the time were religious prose and poetry; fiction was banned as deceitful and wicked until the end of the eighteenth century. The emphasis was on a rational religion in which Man was supposed to accept his lot in life, accept the fact that he could do nothing to guarantee himself an after-life in Heaven, and accept the fact that he could never really know his God.

As might be expected, this philosophy failed to satisfy the need to express the passionate faith and love of God which the majority of Puritans apparently felt. Men like Jonathan Edwards understood this, and constantly preached against the fiercely rational religion of orthodox Puritanism, urging instead a more immediate religious experience in which the soul was raised from the passive role of spectator to that of actor in religion. Reason had to be transcended, it was argued, because of the very fact that it was finite and therefore stood between God the Infinite and Man. According to Edwards, the relationship between Man and God should not be built on reason, which by its very nature made communication with God impossible, but on love, which is the root of all other "affections." The soul must be committed to God *in love,* and this love was impossible as long as orthodoxy refused to allow the soul to know its God. The heart must be affected, he said, else all religion would be mere mouthing of doctrine. Unfortunately, Edwards was misunderstood, and by 1750 he was forced to leave his church in Northampton, Massachusetts; orthodoxy and reason had seemingly prevailed.

With the printed and spoken word in New England under such close scrutiny by the orthodox forces, pictorial symbols were the only remaining means for transcending reason. As Allen Ludwig says in *Graven Images,* "Their love could not be reduced to the cold incision of a name on a boulder, and so, the Puritans fell back upon symbols often older than Christianity itself to express their hopes and fears in the face of the mysteries of death and Resurrection." It should be apparent to us just how great was this need for transcendence if we consider the Puritans' past history of rigid iconoclasm in England, where they destroyed untold numbers of saintly statuary before their departure for the New World. In spite of their institutionalized iconophobia, their need for transcending the here-and-now world was overpowering, and New England gravestones were the means chosen to encourage this transcendence.

It should be noted, however, that New England graveyards and gravestones were never under the direct control of institutionalized religion, and therefore whatever attempts were made to bring the eternal closer through graveyard art were also done outside and in spite of organized religion. Sometimes we find evidence of ministerial control of gravestone images; here and there we may find disfigured stones, where the faces of the soul effigies have been neatly chiseled away. This disfigurement (which is usually too carefully done to be attributed to vandalism) may be regarded as a sort of censorship; if a stonecarver went overboard in his carving and in the process stepped on religious toes, he might well have been prevailed upon to erase the offending image. Such cases are rare, however. For the most part, New England graveyard art enjoyed more freedom from control than did other art forms, and therefore grew out of what was considered proper by the community as a whole. Richly endowed with a mystical symbolism, the graveyard imagery of the early Americans was truly an art of the people, their symbols awakening in them imaginings of after-life that words alone could not express.

⤙ GRAVEYARD SYMBOLS ⤚

Three primary symbol motifs dominate the grave-stones of the Boston area and radiate outward through many of New England's cemeteries. Each of them en-joyed a period of popularity that corresponds fairly well with the predominant religious attitude of its time.

THE DEATH'S-HEAD

The earliest of these motifs was the Elizabethan winged death's-head with its blank eyes and tooth-some grin, a motif often borrowed from broadsides announcing the funerals of prominent persons (see Figs. 1 and 2). Popular in America during the era of staunch orthodox Puritanism from 1620 until approxi-mately 1700, the death's-head was used either by itself or with secondary mortality symbols such as the hour-glass, pick, scythe, or cross-bones. These symbols may be interpreted as graphic illustrations of mortality, em-phasizing life's brevity and the awesome power of Death, and symbolically depicting the soul's voyage through death. This symbolic voyage is especially ap-parent when we see stones carved with a death's-head pierced by a living vine, symbol of life in heaven.

THE SOUL EFFIGY

Gradually, with the decline of orthodox Puritanism that began around 1700, the grim death's-head began to be softened and transformed until, by the 1750's, it had become what we shall call a winged cherub, or soul effigy (see Figs. 3 and 4). Symbolizing Man's immortal side, and suggesting themes of life rather than death, this motif was never as popular in Boston

FIGURE 2: *Winged death's-head on the Elizabeth Adams stone, no date.*
Marblehead, Massachusetts.

24

FIGURE 3: *Winged soul effigy on the William Rogers stone, 1792. Kings Chapel, Boston, Massachusetts.*

proper as was the death's-head, probably because of the still strong influence of Puritan officials. Outside of Boston, however, the cherub–soul effigy flourished, probably becoming the most popular motif of its time.

Epitaphs, too, underwent a gradual change. While the epitaphs on death's-head stones usually began "Here lies the body of . . .," and helped to emphasize the feeling of Man's mortality, those on cherub stones tended to stress the joy of resurrection and immortality; the emphasis had shifted away from death's more fearsome aspects, and toward the idea of a heavenly reward after death.

THE URN-AND-WILLOW

By the beginning of the nineteenth century, religious life had given gradual rise to less emotional, more questioning, and more intellectual sects such as Unitarianism. Accompanying this change came a neo-classicism in the arts that combined with the new religious outlook to yield a new motif—the urn-and-willow (see Fig. 5). The urn, of course, contained the remains of human life from which arise the soul to heaven and was therefore really more sign than symbol. The willow symbolized both mourning for the loss of earthly life and the joy of celestial life. To the casual observer, urn-and-willow stones often seem so nearly identical as to be monotonous; their epitaphs are likely to begin "In memory of . . ." or "Sacred to the memory of . . .," thereby neatly avoiding any discussion of death or eternity. With the introduction of the urn-and-willow, we see a marked and rapid decrease in the number and quality of more inspired stones, and by the mid-1800's we find little but this single design.

FIGURE 4: *Man's soul is immortal: Soul effigies on the Elizabeth Russel stone, 1771. Marblehead, Massachusetts.*

27

FIGURE 5: *The William Clark stone, 1846, displays the urn-and-willow. Marblehead, Massachusetts.*

Although the death's-head, winged cherub, and urn-and-willow stones are the most common and widely found design motifs, countless others deserve mention. In rural New England, as we have seen, the stonecarver was far less influenced by English styles than his city counterpart and so he translated his religious ideas about death into simple, often geometrical, carvings, uncluttered by the baroque curlicues found on many of the urban stones. Figures 6 and 7 are both excellent examples of the fresh inventiveness of the rural carvers. Contrast the simplicity of this style with the urban sophistication of the stones in Figure 10.

Only part of the fun of graveyard "haunting" lies in getting out into the sun and fresh air, and in making with your own hands what can be really beautiful and subtle reproductions of a vanished art (we'll get to that in the next chapter). You'll also find a real sense of excitement and discovery in learning to "read"—almost to decode—the messages about the lives and outlooks of our forebears that have been left for us in the early burial grounds of this country. In addition to the three main symbols discussed above, here is a list of some of the more interesting and revealing symbols, urban and rural, you're likely to find, together with their possible interpretations.

Angels: Easily confused with soul effigies, they symbolize the heavenly host, and are often seen leading the soul towards heaven.

Architectural Symbols: Death is thought of as the "gateway" to heaven; an arch carved on a stone suggests a passageway through which the soul will travel. Sometimes the stones themselves are shaped like

FIGURE 6 (above): *Staring soul effigy contrasts with gay decoration on the Elizabeth Cue stone, 1726, in rural Wenham, Massachusetts.*

FIGURE 7 (opposite): *A country throwback to Puritan grimness: The Bethiah Friend stone, 1765. Wenham, Massachusetts.*

FIGURE 8: *Awake and repent! The cock crows on the Naomi Woolworth stone, 1760. Longmeadow, Massachusetts.*

arches, and are adorned with pillars, drapery, and other architectural devices.

Arrows: In a society ever threatened by death at the hands of Indians, the arrow was a natural symbol for the "dart of death."

Bible: Opened to a page of scripture, it symbolizes the Word through which one gains revelation. This was not a popular symbol in New England, but is seen in many other areas of the country.

Cocks and Peacocks: Peter was awakened from his fall from grace by the crowing of the cock. These vain birds represent not only the fall from grace, but also the awakening to repentance (see Fig. 8).

Coffins and Urns: Symbolic of the death of the flesh, we find many stones carved with a coffin containing a body or soul effigy.

Crowns: Especially popular in the Connecticut River Valley, the crown of righteousness proclaims the victorious soul, arisen to heaven through Christ (see Fig. 9).

Death and Father Time: These two figures are usually found in conjunction with one another, and have a long-standing symbolic tradition. They are often seen struggling over the lighted candle of Life (see Figs. 10a & b).

Dove: Traditionally, the symbol of Christian constancy and devotion.

FIGURE 9 (above): *Crown of righteousness on the Lovice Dunten stone, 1786. Sturbridge, Massachusetts.*

FIGURE 10 (opposite): (A, top) *Father Time and an arrow-wielding Death struggle over life's candle on the Joseph Tapping stone (1678, Kings Chapel, Boston, Massachusetts).* (B, bottom) *Father Time, who has surrendered his scythe to Death, seems to say that Samuel Adams's hour has come, 1728. Kings Chapel, Boston, Massachusetts.*

Flames Arising from the Top of an Urn: The flame represents the soul, arising triumphant out of the ashes of death.

Flowers: Since the time of Christ, flowers have been associated with the life of Man, symbolizing both the beauty and brevity of his life. Sometimes seen is a scythe cutting down the flower (see Fig. 11a), but more often we find only the flower, its stem neatly broken in half (see Fig. 11b).

Geometric Rosettes: Almost always used in conjunction with soul effigies, there are many variations of this design, the most popular of which is the six-pointed rosette. The rosette is sometimes found to have replaced the soul effigy altogether.

Gourds: Popular in the seventeenth and eighteenth centuries, the gourd symbolizes both the coming to be and the passing away of earthly life. Sometimes gourds are carved under soul effigies in fruit columns, and are nearly indistinguishable from breasts (see Fig. 12).

Grapevine: Christ said "I am the true vine," and often the Church is thought of as the vine, and its members the grapes or branches of the vine (see Fig. 13). Sometimes we see soul effigies sucking the ends of grapevines, partaking of the wine which was a major Puritan symbol. A bird sitting in a grapevine, eating the grapes, may symbolize the spirit or soul partaking of celestial food. A vine growing from the top of a skull may be interpreted as the triumph of life over Death and Time.

Heart: The symbol of the soul in heavenly bliss, the

heart is almost always used in direct opposition to some symbol of death.

Heart in the Mouth of a Death's-Head: Symbol of the triumphant soul emerging out of Death.

Heavenly Bodies—the Moon, Stars, and Sun: While these may simply represent the heavenly home of the blessed, they are often used to symbolize the rising of the soul to heaven. A sun is often half-shown, symbolizing both the setting or end of earthy life, and the rising or beginning of heavenly life (see Fig. 14).

Hourglass: Sometimes seen with its own wings, the hourglass is an obvious symbol of the swift passage of Time (see Fig. 15).

Imps of Death: Used mainly by the Lamson family, these naked little men may be armed with the arrows of death, or they may be busy at some task, such as lowering a coffin into the grave, symbolic of the triumph of Death (see Fig. 16).

Portraits: Often we see actual portraits carved in stone (see Fig. 17a), and sometimes a facial portrait borne upwards on feathered wings. These may be considered a form of soul effigy, or in some cases, a symbol of the deceased's position in life (see Fig. 17b). See also *Station-in-Life Symbols*.

Profile Soul Effigy in the Mouth of a Death's-Head: Once again, a symbol of the soul arising triumphant out of Death.

Scallop Shell: This is the traditional symbol of the Pilgrims' crusade, and of Man's earthly pilgrimage.

FIGURE 11 (opposite): (A, top) *The flower of life is cut by a scythe on Eunice Colton's stone (1763. Long-meadow, Massachusetts), and (B, bottom) broken neatly on the Lucy Harris stone, 1780, in Marblehead, Massachusetts.*

FIGURE 12 (left): *The Rebeckah Whitmore stone (1709. Lexington, Massachusetts) displays gourds, or perhaps breasts—both symbols of earthly life and vitality.*

FIGURE 13 (below): *That Pamela Munro (1770. Lexington, Massachusetts) was a faithful daughter of the Church is symbolized by a grapevine. The birds may represent the soul eating celestial food.*

FIGURE 14 (top): *Both the end of earthly life and beginning of heavenly life are represented by a setting—or rising—sun on the Mary Tarbox stone, 1792. Wenham, Massachusetts.*

FIGURE 15: *The winged hourglass: Swift-flying time alights briefly on the head of a soul effigy, on the Captain John Chapham stone, 1761. Lexington, Massachusetts.*

FIGURE 16: *An Imp of Death slides a glance at a mournful admonition as he lowers a shrouded form in the grave, on the Rebeckah Whitmore stone, 1709. Lexington, Massachusetts.*

Scythe: Usually seen in the hands of Father Time, the scythe cuts Man's life short.

Station-in-Life Symbols: Indicating the rank or occupation of the deceased, these symbols include coats-of-arms, military insignia, ships, etc. (see Figs. 17b, 18, and 19).

Symbols of the Cause of Death: These stones are interesting in that the carvings portray how the person died. For instance, in Groton, Mass., there is a stone which shows a body underneath a fallen tree, with the inscription "Died by a falling tree."

Symbols of the Soul in Flight: Winged soul effigies may be thought of as souls in flight towards heaven; flying birds, symbolic of the soul, also have this connotation.

Tree of Life: Symbolizing either earthly or heavenly life, as well as spiritual values, the tree of life was

FIGURE 17: *Facial portraits of the deceased appear* (A) *on the Anna Barnard stone* (1774. *Marblehead, Massachusetts) and* (B) *indicate the*

social station of the Rev. Nathaniel Rogers (1775. Ipswich, Massachu-setts).

FIGURE 18: *Station-in-life is shown by the ornate coat of arms on the M. Bartholomew Gedney stone, no date. Kings Chapel, Boston, Massachusetts.*

FIGURE 19: A *seaman goes to God: the ship* Trumbull *on the Jabez Smith stone, 1780. The Granary, Boston, Massachusetts.*

45

especially popular during the 1700's and was used in poetic imagery as well as on gravestones.

Trumpeting Figures: Often carrying a banner which reads "Arise ye dead," this may be interpreted as the "last trump that rends the skies," calling all of the faithful departed to their final Resurrection. See the Elizabeth Nichols and Mary Cumings stones (Figs. 20a and b) for good examples. If you look closely at the Cumings stone, you will notice that "Arise ye dead" has been written backwards in the banner. Just how this happened is anyone's guess, but my theory is that an illiterate apprentice to the stonecarver traced the design on backwards, and had started carving before anyone realized what had happened, leaving no other alternative but to finish backwards. Or perhaps, as one gentleman suggested, the backwards motif was meant to be appreciated not by those of us who stand outside the stone, but by some spirit within the stone.

Urns-and-Mermaids: Mermaids are traditionally thought of as symbolizing a dual nature; the mermaids of ancient literature were often depicted as sirens whose function it was to bring souls to Proserpina. On New England gravestones, mermaids may be seen carrying the urns containing the mortal remains of the deceased, symbolizing the last step of our earthly journey (see Fig. 21). See also *Coffins and Urns.*

Wine, the Divine Fluid: Sacramental tankards or chalices were used to symbolize the soul's partaking of heavenly bliss, but interestingly, we find these only on the stones of deacons of the church. See also *Grape-vine.*

The foregoing list of graveyard symbols is not, of

FIGURE 20: *The last trump sounds* (A, top) *on the Elizabeth Nichols stone* (1778. *Wakefield, Massachusetts*) *and in reverse* (B) *on the Mary Cumings stone* (1790. *Billerica, Massachusetts*).

47

FIGURE 21: *Mermaids carry a funeral urn on Timothy Dwyt's stone, 1691/2. The Granary, Boston, Massachusetts.*

course, complete. Throughout New England, and even more so in other areas of the country, you will find symbols and combinations of symbols that have not been discussed here. In most cases, however, unusual designs sprang from the inspiration of a single stonecarver, and will be seen only on stones carved by him.

One of my favorite stones in terms of symbolic imagery is the Susanna Jayne stone in Marblehead, Massachusetts (see Fig. 22). Encircled by a hooped snake, symbolic of eternity, Death victorious stands crowned by a laurel wreath and draped in winding sheets, holding the twin orbs of the sun and moon in his hands. In opposition with one another are the bats of the lower corners (symbolizing the evils of this life and the perils of death) and the cherubs of the upper corners (symbolizing the goodness of life here-

48

FIGURE 22: *Rich symbolism (interpreted in the text on pages 48 and 51) embellishes the Marblehead, Massachusetts, stone of Susanna Jayne, 1776.*

FIGURE 23: *The grim, apparently Puritan front* (A, top) *of the Elizabeth Katherin Gwin Sharp stone* (undated) *in Boston's Kings Chapel burial ground is alleviated by the back's delightful copy-book mix* (B) *of curlicues, alphabets, and partial designs; the stonecutter evidently used a practice stone.*

after). At the top of the stone are two traditional mortality symbols, the hourglass and bones. Cut in 1776 by Henry Christian Geyer of Boston, this stone is beautifully carved and has been well cared for by Marblehead's cemetery officials; it is a fine example of early New England stonecarving.

Another stone, which I find especially fascinating, is the Elizabeth Katherin Gwin Sharp stone in the King's Chapel graveyard, Boston (see Figs. 23a and b). A small stone with no date, the front of the stone is carved with the standard death's-head and name; on the back are odd curlicues, parts of designs, an alphabet, and a tiny upside-down death's-head. Apparently this stone was once used as a practice stone by some early carver; I imagine that it was used here as the footstone rather than the more important headstone for the grave. It seems to have been a common practice to carve footstones out of whatever was handy at the moment, even though they might not match their headstones. That is certainly the case here.

For a further explanation of graveyard art, take a look at Allen Ludwig's *Graven Images*, a very scholarly and detailed work, and well worth reading.

EARLY NEW ENGLAND GRAVESTONES AND STONECUTTERS

Throughout New England, the very earliest grave markers you will see were made of raw fieldstone, adorned only with crudely carved initials and a date (see Fig. 24). By the 1650's, the stonecutting art had advanced, and the artists were using stones finished on at least one side to make carving easier. At this time, stonecarvers were using heavy, horizontal guidelines for their letters, and "suspended periods" between words (see Fig. 25). Traditionally, it was thought that these later, more carefully planed and carved stones were brought from England as ship's ballast. However, this was probably not the case. As early as 1654, the Hayden Stone Pit in Windsor, Connecticut, was in full operation, and well before 1700, slate quarries were operational in Massachusetts. Furthermore, there are no ships' records of gravestones having been used as ballast, nor are there merchants' records of stones having been purchased from English sources. Also, there are many letters on record from American families to American stonecutters, ordering gravestones to be cut. Geologists, too, have helped to invalidate the English-import theory by identifying many gravestones as having come from local areas. With this evidence, as well as the knowledge that there were, at that time, men in America capable of both mining and carving gravestones, we can safely say that, with few exceptions, New England's stones were of local origin.

Of course, the type of stone used varied from region to region, according to what was available from the local quarries. In and around Boston a fine slate was abundant, while in other regions the carvers had to make do with poor schists which cracked and split easily. Throughout the Connecticut River Valley quarries produced lovely red standstones of highly durable quality, and even today, two-hundred-and-fifty-year-old gravestones carved of this material still look freshly cut. It was not until sometime towards the late 1700's that marble began to gain popularity. Used extensively throughout Vermont by talented carvers like Zerubbabel Collins, these marble stones rival in quality the best of the slates and sandstones found in more southern regions. Fieldstone, which we

FIGURE 24: *The E L stone, 1647. Ipswich, Massachusetts.*

FIGURE 25: *This drawing of the Sarah [Hammond?] stone, 1674, shows early Puritan stonecutting style: heavy lettering, suspended periods, horizontal guidelines. Watertown, Massachusetts.*

have already mentioned, was of course used everywhere for the more modest stones, as this term simply refers to any rough stone taken from the fields. Naturally, fiieldstone is of every type or variety found in a given locale.

Gravestone motif styles are found to vary greatly between urban-coastal and rural locales, reflecting the differences between English and American art. In coastal Boston, for instance, ships were constantly arriving from England, bringing with them a wealth of information on the latest fashions in England. Remembering that at this time the inhabitants of New England still considered themselves Englishmen, it should not surprise us that they tried to keep up with English styles as much as possible. Though New England's coastal design styles were perhaps fifty years behind those of England, these trends have been definitely traced to England.

In rural areas, however, the English stylistic influence was not nearly as great, and the local craftsmen were left to their own inventiveness. Their designs were more abstract and "primitive" and they tended to rely heavily on nature as a source of inspiration. More linear than modeled, their motifs may be considered a far more spontaneous, purely American art form than those of the coastal carvers. It was not until well into the 1800's that the rural designs finally began to give way to the English-inspired sterility of the urn-and-willow.

NOTABLE STONECUTTERS

One of the problems in the study of graveyard art is that it was not a conscious art form—the men who carved the stones did not keep records of them, nor did they keep sketch books of ideas for the designs. When their diaries mention carving a stone, it is usually only the name, date, and price of the stone that is recorded. Although it is possible that some stonecarvers may have brought their designs with them from England, this is rather doubtful since there are no records of any practicing English carvers coming to this country. Most of our early stonecarvers were men who made their livings as woodcarvers, masons, or leatherworkers; they became stonecarvers only when the need arose. Perhaps, had New England stonecarvers thought of themselves more as true artists than as simple craftsmen, they would have left us more details concerning the origins and uses of their designs.

With a few notable exceptions, stones of a particular style are usually the work of one man. Sometimes an apprentice might copy that style for a few years, but eventually he would branch out to develop a distinctive style of his own. With experience one can trace the work of a given stonecarver throughout various graveyards. Although the work of exceedingly well-known and popular stonecarvers may be found throughout much of New England, for the most part gravestones were produced locally, and the work of any one man was usually confined to an area centered on his home. Few of these locally produced stones have been moved since the time of their original emplacement, except within the confines of the graveyard.

As the population of America grew, so did the need for skilled stonecarvers, so that by 1700 there were at least fifty stonecarvers in the Boston area alone. Here we find that the work of the Lamson family is probably the most famous. A cordwainer, surveyor, and mariner, Joseph Lamson also cut stones and fathered a line of sons who followed in his footsteps. Characteristics of Lamson stones include the little naked imps of death, drapery across the tops of stones, death's-heads with broad foreheads and highly curved

FIGURE 26: *A typical Lamson death's-head.*

FIGURE 27: *An early Stevens death's-head.*

FIGURE 28: *A Wright face.*

eyebrows (see Fig. 26), and heads or soul effigies at the tops of fruit columns. Lamson is also notable as being one of the first stonecarvers to use lower case letters as frequently as capitals. Sometimes, we are lucky enough to find stones initialled J.L. and these we can be fairly certain are true Lamson stones.

In Rhode Island, the family of stonecutters founded by John Stevens is among the best known. We know little about the first fifty years of John's life, but we do know that his first son was born when he was fifty-five, and that thereafter he had another six children. His son John also became a noted stonecarver, and it is from John's journal that we glean most of the information about this family. Their simpler stones are characterized by death's-heads with hanging teeth (see Fig. 27) and a simple border, usually of rosettes connected by a cord or vine. While the younger Stevens learned his trade from his father, his taste in motifs tended more toward little cherubs with wings above their heads. The second Stevens is also known to have carved many of the armorial slabs found in Newport. This stonecutting tradition continued from father to son until finally in 1900, with some 200 years of carving behind him, the last of the Stevens stonecutters died.

An early stonecutter in Connecticut, and one who kept a diary, was Joshua Hempstead. A man of many talents, he held several town offices such as executor of wills, guardian of widows and orphans, and so on, and he was also known to be a mariner, surveyor, attorney, and carpenter, as well as stonecutter. His diary gives us a good deal of information concerning stone-carving of the day, the cost of raw stones, the techniques of carving, the price of finished stones. Oddly, he did not mention stonecarving until he was forty-two years old, and even then he did not mention where he learned the trade, or why. He has two distinct styles, the first being simply lettered stones with no ornamentation, carved on red sandstone. His other stones are carved of a grey stone, are simply lettered, and include a poorly carved conventional border. It does not seem that he was interested so much in technique as in speed of carving. Joshua Hempstead died in the mid-1700's, leaving behind him many stones and probably one of the finest and most useful of diaries.

In Vermont, we find the work of the Wright family to be of special interest. Working on a tight-grained black slate, the Wrights carved highly imaginative images using fine lines and working with a compass to achieve the perfectly round faces that are their hallmark (see Fig. 28). Rockingham abounds with Wright faces such as these, and in Chester we find the famous Lucinda Day stone, with its round face peering out of the feathered chest of an eagle. (Rubbings of this stone and of the Park family stone appear in the last section of this book.) As with most Vermont carvers, the Wright style was highly individualistic and once perfected, changed very little.

The works of these and many other talented stonecarvers are still to be seen and admired in graveyards throughout New England.

2. Rubbing

RUBBING, the modern word referring to the ancient Chinese art of *"T'a-pen,"* or "ink-squeezing," is primarily a means of reproducing a design or motif carved on any rubbable surface such as stone, wood, or plaster. By placing paper over the surface of the image to be copied, and rubbing with an ink or wax, a negative print of the image is produced.

The technique of rubbing originated in China, where the earliest rubbing still in existence dates back to the seventh century A.D. There is no record, however, of how long before then the art actually began. It is known that in many instances rubbing was used as an early method of making multiple copies before the advent of the printing press; and there is some evidence to show that Buddhist and Confucian texts were carved in stone for the purpose of "printing" books. The practice of doing rubbings as a form of publishing is known to have existed as far back as 1200 A.D.

The early T'a-pen artists used a multi-layered rice paper, which they dampened with a plant or mineral-salt solution and laid over the surface to be rubbed, pressing the paper down so that it adhered to the surface of the stone. They used specially prepared inks composed of carbon and mineral oils, combined with glue, molded into stick shapes, and then dried. Called *Sumi* ink by the Japanese, these sticks, when ground and mixed with water, produced an ink very much like

FIGURE 29: T'a-pen: *a Thai rubbing using* Sumi *inks freezes the dancers'*
grace.

61

FIGURE 30: T'a-pen: *horses prance in this* Sumi *ink rubbing from Thailand.*

our present-day India ink. *Tampos,* or dabbers made of balls of cotton wrapped with layers of oiled cloth and covered finally with fine silk, were used to apply the ink to the paper. When dry, the rubbing was removed from the stone, a finished work of art (see Figs. 29 and 30).

An intriguing outcropping of T'a-pen was the art of *Gyotaku,* a technique of inking a fish and making an impression of it on paper (see Fig. 31). Until the advent and ready availability of photographic equipment, this was the only means available of recording the size and type of a prize catch. Though the origin of this art is still unknown, fish prints dating from 1862 have been discovered in private collections in Japan.

The art of rubbing was very slow to catch on in the West, where the earliest examples may have dated back to the early twelfth century, though none of these has survived to the present day. The most significant rubbings of the Western culture were taken from monumental brasses—figures or inscriptions engraved in brass and placed in churches throughout

FIGURE 31: *He didn't get away! In Gyotaku, a fish is inked and pressed to the paper to produce a remarkably delicate print—and to record the catch.*

central Europe and the British Isles to commemorate the dead. Often lifesize, the earliest of these brasses were done in the late thirteenth century, and the last were done in the middle of this century (see Fig. 32). The art of brass rubbing reached its zenith in the middle of the fourteenth century, flourished for a while, and then all but disappeared until its revival about ten years ago. Today, brass rubbing has become so popular that many churches have found it necessary to charge a fee, while some have even limited rubbing to professionals.

In the United States, rubbing was never a truly popular art until the late 1960's. Until then it was used almost exclusively by craftsmen: stonecarvers who needed to transfer the design of one stone to another; professional artists; or archaeologists who wished to record ancient carvings. Although in many cases the art of rubbing has been replaced by photography, rubbing still gives the most accurate reproductions of the minute detail on many of the ancient carvings.

Today, however, rubbing is becoming increasingly popular throughout the United States and especially in the historical New England area, where numerous gravestones of early colonial times are easily accessible. All sorts of people are found doing rubbings: history teachers seeking interesting and authentic materials for their classes; young people who want to create significant, conversation-provoking "posters" for their apartments; men and women who are tracing their family trees and wish to have tangible evidences of their ancestors. Courses in rubbing techniques and gravestone symbolism have begun to appear at universities and community colleges; local historical societies and museums are beginning to collect rubbings of these stones which are so much a part of our

FIGURE 32: *A typical brass rubbing, from England.*

early heritage. Unquestionably, gravestone rubbing is becoming a very popular art which, as it is relatively easy and requires but a few simple and inexpensive tools, is being taken up by an astonishingly large number of enthusiasts.

RUBBING TECHNIQUES

In this section, I'll talk about four basic rubbing techniques that should enable you, once you've mastered them, to "capture" just about any kind of stone. They are: the Dry Method, which I use on almost all slate stones (slate is generally found to be smooth) except those delicately incised; the Carbon Paper Method, especially good for delicately incised slate; the Dabbing, or Wet, Method, which is almost a "must" for sandstone or weathered marble (which can often be grainy) though it can also be used on slate; and the Foil and Plaster Cast Method, which is fun and works on almost any stone.

The first step in each of these is the same—that is, to survey the graveyard and to find a stone that you like and that is suitable for your rubbing technique. I find that whenever I go into a graveyard, intent upon doing some rubbings, I cannot help but walk through the whole yard, looking at each stone. By the time I've seen them all, I've forgotten where some of the best stones were. This was always a problem, especially in large, not very well organized yards, until I started taking along some children's modeling clay and some small, brightly colored flags. Now, when I find a stone I like, I put a lump of clay on top of it and stick in a flag, making it easy to find again when I am ready to do the rubbing of it.

You may wish to take a Polaroid camera along with you to take pictures of the stones before you begin your rubbings. Once your rubbing is in progress, you may find that you don't remember some of the details of the stone; your Polaroid photo will provide a ready reference for you. You can also use these photos in a simple catalogue system to help you keep track of your rubbings. Write all pertinent information—town, date, location of stone in cemetery, etc.—on the back of the photo, and then file it away. While this may not seem necessary at first, the more towns you visit and rubbings you do, the more you will begin to get them mixed up. When your visiting aunt decides there is nothing she wants more than a copy of your favorite rubbing—the one in the expensive frame on your living room wall—you will want to be able to go do another one just for her. What a shame if, by that time, you've forgotten where it came from!

When you go out to do your rubbings, remember to take along an old towel or pillow to kneel on. This will help protect you from ants and dirt, and will provide an excellent cushion for weary knees.

CLEANING STONES

You will also need to take along a stiff brush or an eraser for cleaning the stones of moss, bird droppings, and especially lichen. Lichen, in order to hold onto the stone, secretes an enzyme that erodes the surface of the stone, and as it spreads and grows, it naturally destroys increasingly large areas. One of the best things you can do to help preserve a gravestone is to remove this lichen from it. This can be accomplished by using either a fairly stiff (but *not* wire) bristle brush, or an eraser. You must take care, however, not to be too rough, or *you* will damage the stone. Most impurities will flake off easily. If they don't, then just leave them, smoothing them down as much as possible. They will not harm your rubbing.

THE DRY METHOD

I use the dry method on all slate stones except the most delicately incised. It is by far the easiest and most foolproof method I have found of doing rubbings. Materials you will need for it include:

> A brush or eraser for cleaning the stone
> Paper (fairly lightweight but tear-resistant—I prefer aqaba, but many people use rice, mulberry, and even architect's drafting paper with good results)
> Scissors or knife for cutting paper, weeds, etc.
> Masking tape
> Rubbing media (crayon, charcoal, graphite, wax)
> Spray fixative (for soft media, like charcoal or graphite)
> A cloth or Wash n' Dry for cleaning your hands
> Cardboard tube or portfolio for storing paper and finished rubbings

For your first rubbings, choose smooth-surfaced, dark stones with clearly engraved lettering, and not too much relief in the motif. Urn-and-willow stones are almost always a good choice for this purpose. Later on you can go to more difficult stones, such as those with rough texture or a great deal of erosion. Such stones are often the basis for the most interesting rubbings.

If there is anything on the surface of the stone you have chosen, use your brush or eraser to clean it off. Proceed *gently*, so as not to harm the stone.

After the stone is clean, tear off several pieces of masking tape and place them so that they are easily accessible. Center the paper on the front of the stone; then, holding it in place with one hand, tape it to the stone with the other. The first piece of tape should securely fasten the center of the top edge; the second should anchor the bottom center. After these are firmly attached, make sure that the paper is as tight as possible across the face of the stone, and then put as many other pieces of tape on as are necessary to hold the paper securely in place when you begin to rub. Slipping paper during the rubbing process will surely ruin an otherwise excellent rubbing.

The next step is to block in the design of your rubbing. Using the broadest expanse of your rubbing medium (which I will refer to as wax in these instructions), rub gently across the paper in large sweeping motions. Wherever the paper comes into contact with the surface of the stone beneath, your wax will adhere. Cutaway areas will remain white. You will

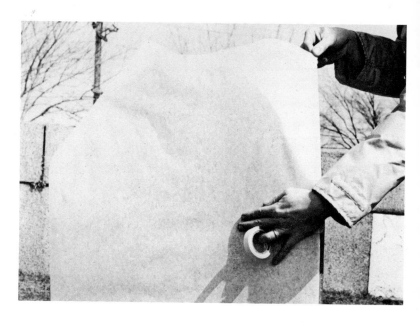

FIGURE 33: *Tape the paper securely to the stone.*

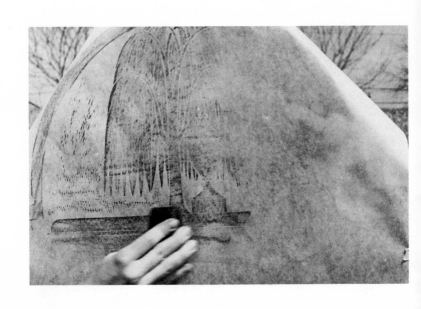

FIGURE 34: *Block in the basic design with a broad, flat edge of your wax.*

want to be especially careful not to let your wax slip
into these white areas; slipping will leave unwanted
marks across them, and will disfigure the rubbing.
This is another reason for choosing an urn-and-willow
stone, for very often it will be almost entirely covered
by design-work, thus eliminating most of the dangerous white areas. However, to be sure of yourself, you
can refer to your Polaroid snapshot, or you can feel
the engraving through the paper. The more rubbings
you do, the more sensitive your fingers will become to
the feeling of a stone, so that eventually you will be
able to detect even the smallest of these danger areas
by touch.

Having blocked in the design, begin to fill it in,
rubbing more firmly across the paper with your wax.
This will take a little time and patience, though it is
not difficult. As you work, your wax will develop sharp
corners and straight edges. Use them! The sharp
corners will enable you to get into corners and small
spaces in the engraved design. The straight edges are
very handy for rubbing over lettering, where you need
a broad enough piece of wax so that you can rub across
the entire letter without leaving marks inside it. When
you are working around letters, be sure to rub in the
direction of the slant of the letters in order to avoid
catching chunks of your wax on the letter edges.

Your rubbing is finished as soon as its clarity and
darkness suit you. Remember that what looks very
dark in the bright sunlight will look much lighter in
the artificial light of your home, so it is a good idea to
make your rubbing somewhat darker than you think
you want it. After you have done a few rubbings, you
will be able to judge their darkness, and this precau-
tion will no longer be necessary. Before you take your
rubbing off the stone, stand back and take a good look
at it. You may see things from a distance that you

FIGURE 35: *Darken the rubbing until its color suits you.*

failed to notice close up, and that you will want to change. You may also find that there are what appear to be light streaks through an otherwise evenly darkened rubbing. These are caused by rubbing in different directions, so that the wax reflects light at different angles. To eliminate these streaks, re-rub the entire rubbing very lightly, using vertical strokes only. Now, if you are happy with it, your rubbing is finished, and you can take it off the stone, being very careful not to tear the paper when you remove the tape from it.

If you have used a soft medium like charcoal or graphite, you will want to spray it with fixative *immediately*, thus preventing any possibility of smearing. If you have used a more permanent medium, you can handle your rubbing immediately using only ordinary care.

When you get home with your rubbings, you may want to add some finishing touches. Where imperfections in the stone have shown up in the rubbing, very careful retouching with the original medium may erase them. On the other hand, imperfections from the stone give each rubbing a character of its own, and you may wish to leave them. If your medium has caked anywhere on the rubbing, as often happens with most waxes and crayons on hot days, the excess can be removed by letting the rubbing cool thoroughly, then using a sharp razor or knife and simply shaving across the surface of the rubbing. If you have used a smear-proof medium like hard wax, you may want to bring out a shine in your rubbing by buffing it with a piece of old, well-worn and softened brown-paper bag. I prefer paper bag to almost any cloth, since it has very little texture of its own to mar the texture of the rubbing. When mounting your rubbings for display, a sheet of heavy white paper used as backing will help to heighten the contrast of the rubbing.

FIGURE 36: *Detail of the finished dry rubbing.*

Many media are available for this method. Until a few years ago, the best of these, in my opinion, was English Heel Ball, a very hard wax made of carnauba and lampblack, which had to be imported from England. (This is not to be confused with heel ball produced in the United States, which is very soft, has low pigment content, and gives generally poor rubbings.) Now, however, there are American-made waxes which are equally as good as the imported ones. Of these, my favorites, which I use for nearly all of my rubbings, are the Oldstone Enterprises waxes; they are available in several excellent colors and are easily obtainable at most art stores. You may find that you prefer different media for different weather conditions. I have found that the hotter it gets, the more I enjoy working with a very hard wax. As it gets colder, on the other hand, I prefer the softer waxes, as these do not become so brittle and therefore remain easier to work with. I hardly ever resort to graphite or charcoal, however, for the simple reason that they are much too messy to work with and do nothing to improve the quality of my rubbings.

❧ THE CARBON PAPER
METHOD ❧

This method is just about as easy as the dry method, although it is messier. It is especially well suited to rubbings of smooth stones with very intricately engraved motifs, since carbon paper rubbings record a great deal of very delicately incised detail. Your material for this method should include:

Rubbing paper (very lightweight rice paper or tracing paper)
Scissors
Masking tape
Spray bottle filled with water
Ordinary carbon paper
Newsprint
Pieces of old shoe leather (large enough to hold onto easily) or a bamboo rice paddle
Spray fixative
Cloth for cleaning your hands
Cardboard tube or portfolio for storing paper and finished rubbings

Carefully clean the stone as discussed earlier, then tape your rubbing paper to it as explained in the dry method. When the paper is secured, spray it with water. Since you are using very lightweight paper, it will sag as it gets wet; *gently* remove the tape from the stone and *very gently* pull the paper tighter, resticking the tape to the stone. As you see the need, add more pieces of tape, before the paper is dry, to make certain that it will be held firmly in place. When the paper is fully dry, it will contract and pull tightly across the face of the stone.

When the rubbing paper is dry, take a large sheet of newsprint and tape it securely to the top back edge

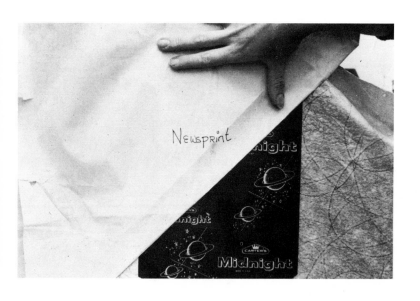

FIGURE 37: *Tape your good paper to the stone. Tape the newsprint so that it hangs over the front of the stone and over the good paper. Place your carbon paper, face down, between the newsprint and the good paper.*

FIGURE 38: *Detail of the finished carbon paper rubbing.*

of the stone so that it hangs down over the front of the stone, covering your rubbing paper. Do not tape the newsprint to the rubbing paper itself. When you have the newsprint in place, take a sheet of carbon paper and place it, carbon side toward the stone, between the rubbing paper and the newsprint.

A *word of caution:* Since you are using very thin, fragile papers, it will be easy to tear through one or all of them, especially the rubbing paper if it is at all wet. Wait for it to dry, and don't be too rough.

Now, if all layers are dry and securely in place, you are ready to rub. Hold all three sheets in place with one hand, and with the other rub all three layers of paper at once. A piece of old shoe leather or a bamboo rice paddle is ideal for rubbing with. When you have completed this carboning process on one section of the stone, you may lift the newsprint and relocate your carbon paper. The only paper which must not move is the rubbing paper itself. However, when you have done one area and are working on the next, be careful not to let the newsprint slip or slide against the finished area, as this will smear the carbon on the rubbing. You may wish to do one area and then spray it with fixative before going on to the next.

Your carbon paper rubbing will not be as dark as a dry method rubbing, but it will give you fine clarity of detail. When you are finished, and before the rubbing is removed from the stone, spray it with fixative. It can then be safely handled, rolled up, and stored.

✑ THE DABBING, OR WET, METHOD ↠

This method is essential for sandstone or weathered marble, and it can be used on slate, too. It is more difficult to master than the previous methods, requiring several practice rubbings before satisfactory results will be attained. It is also messier, requiring more special preparation and materials. Materials you will need include:

Japanese rice paper, fairly lightweight but of good quality

Either of the following: 1) water and methylcellulose solution in a spray bottle (to be used *only* on slate stones); or 2) clear water in a spray bottle (to be used on granular, porous stones) (see why just below)

Damp "velour" type terrycloth towel or wash cloth

Water-soluble ink or liquid watercolor*

A shallow dish or jar lid

Tampos or dabbers

Cardboard tube or portfolio for storing paper and finished dabbings

A cloth and clear water for cleaning the stone and your hands

A *word of explanation and caution:* Methylcellulose is a kind of glue; if you use it on sandstone, weathered

---

* Many graveyard officials have banned the use of oil and dye-base inks in their yards due to the permanent stains caused by careless use of such inks. Even the expert can make mistakes, and unwittingly deface a stone. For this reason I use only water-soluble printing inks and watercolors, my favorites being watercolors that come in tubes. Not only can I create an infinite variety of colors with them, but also they are easy to mix with water, forming a soupy paste of my favorite consistency. And when they soak through the paper onto stone, as they invariably do upon occasion, I can simply spray on a little clear water and wash them off again. And please remember to be especially careful when working on porous stones such as sandstone and marble. If you use too much ink, the stone will gladly soak it up, and you will have to spend the next half hour or so with spray bottle and sponge, first flushing the spot with water and then carefully soaking it up in the sponge, until the entire spot is removed. You cannot expect to be sloppy and still be allowed to do more rubbings.

marble, or other coarse-grained stones, your rubbing paper will stick to the stone. When you try to pull the paper off, two things are liable to happen: 1) your paper will tear, and 2) some of the stone will come along with the paper, causing irremediable damage. So be sure you know what kind of stone you are dealing with before you proceed.

As with previous methods, choose your stone and clean it carefully. When the stone is ready, center your paper on the stone and tape it in one or two places so that it is held lightly in position.

Now you are ready to spray it with the water (and methylcellulose, if you are using it; it is easily obtainable in many pharmacies, and is available in either tablet or powder form. To use, dissolve about one teaspoonful of powder in a pint of warm water). Methylcellulose acts not only as a glue but as a contraction agent, and will cause the paper to draw tight and adhere to the stone. I like to spray just a small area at a time, beginning at the center of the motif and working outwards. First spray a little area, then, with your dampened terry towel, *gently* pat the paper, making it adhere to the contours of the stone. Make sure that you have worked out all air bubbles and that there are as few wrinkles in the paper as possible. Continue working, area by area, always radiating outwards, until the entire area to be dabbed is pressed to the stone. This step is very important to the success of your dabbing, so take as much time as you need to do it correctly.

Now let the paper dry somewhat. How wet you want it to be is dependent not only on your dabbing medium, but also on your own preferences based on experience. Generally, if you are using a fairly dry, thick medium, you will want fairly wet paper; if you

FIGURE 39: *Spray the paper a little at a time, and press it to the stone with a dampened terrycloth towel.*

FIGURE 40: *You can make these dabbers yourself.*

are using a thin, wet medium, you will want your paper dry or nearly dry.

While your paper is drying, you can arrange your other materials for easy accessibility during the dabbing process. The dabbing medium (I will call it ink) will be applied with the tampos or dabbers, which you can easily make yourself. To make them, take varying sizes of sponge balls, and cover them, first with two or three layers of muslin, and then with a layer or two of silk. Make sure that the outside covering is pulled fairly taut and smooth around them; if it is loose and lumpy, the dabber will not work well and will cause unevenness in your ink coverage. Be sure to tie the dabbers very tightly around the neck so that there is no chance of their coming loose while you are using them. You'll find it handy, eventually, to have two sizes: a large one for broad, uncarved expanses, and a small one for the tricky, carved-out areas. Experience will show you what you need.

When your paper is ready, pour some of your ink into a shallow bowl or jar lid. With your tampo, soak up some of the ink, and then squeeze off the excess along the lip of the dish. If your tampo has too much ink on it, you will get unsightly blots on your paper. It is better to start out with too little ink, and then to add more as you get used to the method and to your paper. If you are at all unsure of how much ink you have on your tampo, test it on a piece of scrap paper before using it on your good dabbing paper.

Your tampo inked, you can now begin your dabbing. There are two cardinal rules to remember here. The first is, *do not rub* as with the dry method. As the name "dabbing" suggests, brush gently or lightly pat the paper with the inked tampo. Secondly, *do not let the tampo rest on the paper*, as this will cause blotting on your paper as well as on the stone beneath. When

FIGURE 41: *Remember to squeeze excess ink off the dabber before you touch it to the paper.*

FIGURE 42: *Detail of the finished dabbing.*

you run out of ink on your tampo, repeat the inking procedure, remembering to remove the excess ink on the lip of the bowl.

As with the dry method rubbings, there will be dangerous areas around which you will need to be careful. These will show up well, since the paper has adhered to the contours of the stone, so that you needn't worry about slipping into one because you couldn't see it. Such areas are the blank eyes of a death's-head and the carved-out spaces within letters. Use one of your smaller dabbers in these areas, and work carefully around the outside edges, taking care not to smudge.

When your dabbing is done, allow the paper and ink to dry completely, then carefully remove it from the stone, pulling it off with an even, gentle motion. You may then roll it up for easy transportation without fear of smearing it.

ᴗ§ THE FOIL AND PLASTER
CAST METHOD ൠ

The foil method of rubbing is one of my favorites, as it produces an identical replica of the gravestone when done properly. The basic technique is one of etching your foil so that it has the same contours as the stone you are working on, and then turning that foil into a mold, into which you will pour plaster, forming a plaster copy of the stone.

Materials you will need are:

Heavy-duty aluminum foil to tool and make mold from

Assorted sizes of dowels with rounded ends (or small paintbrush handles)

Masking tape

A dry, soft sponge

Scissors

A bowl and spatula for mixing plaster of Paris

Plaster of Paris

Paint or other finish for plaster cast

Epoxy glue and/or decorative wood screws

Wooden plaque to mount casting on

In the graveyard: To begin, clean the stone you have chosen as in previous methods, then cut off a piece of your foil and place it over the surface of the stone, taping it securely, but not too tightly, to the stone. Once the foil is in place, begin to rub with the soft sponge to reveal the general outlines of the stone's motif. Be sure to work from the center outwards, so that any excess foil will end up at the edges of the rubbing, and can then be folded over, out of the way. This is much the same as the blocking in process in the dry method rubbing.

FIGURE 43: *Lightly tape the foil to the stone.*

FIGURE 44: *Using rounded dowels, shape the foil to the contours of the stone.*

FIGURE 45: *Your foil should look like this before you remove it from the stone.*

Having defined the basic outlines of the motif with the sponge, repeat the procedure with the cushions of the tips of your fingers. I suggest using your fingers because then you will be able to feel the design more easily than when working through the sponge. Once the design is established to your satisfaction, begin rubbing with the ends of the rounded dowels. I usually use the ends of small paint brushes, since there are always lots of different shapes and sizes lying around the house, and they are already rounded for me. Be sure to have a variety of sizes of tools with you so that you will be able to get into the smallest carved spaces, and at the same time, have tools large enough to make bold impressions. When rubbing with your tools, *be gentle*, or you will tear your foil; a hole in the foil can be repaired (and should be, or the plaster may leak out), but it is easier not to have to.

Work patiently and slowly until the foil has taken on the exact contours of the stone beneath it. When you are finished with this etching process, and before you remove the foil from the stone, place small patches of tape over any holes you have made in the foil. Then carefully lift the foil from the stone. As soon as possible, get your contoured foil into a protected area, out of the wind, which can batter it in a moment. When you are carrying the foil rubbing, do not try to hold it against the breeze; instead, let it float on the wind. While this may cause the outer edges to bend, it will not endanger the etching itself.

At home: It is now time to turn your completed etching into a mold which will hold the plaster of Paris. Carefully cut away any excess foil, leaving a two- or three-inch edge around all the sides of the etching. With the convex side of the mold lying on your work surface, fold all the edges up—that is, in the

FIGURE 46: *Turn up the edges of the foil and tape the corners tightly to form a mold.*

same direction as the fold you created when you taped the foil to the stone. Join the corners and tape them. If you are, as in Figures 44–46, casting a stone with a curved top, fold the bottom edge up, and join it to the top curved edge, forming corners at the bottom, and securely taping them. This will form a sort of shallow pan, with the etching face down on the bottom, and will serve as your mold. Now, very carefully, being sure not to damage or dent the etched foil, place tape over any holes you may have missed earlier, placing the tape on the bottom *outside* of the mold. (If you place it on the inside, the texture of the tape will be picked up in your plaster cast.)

Now that your mold is ready, place it on a flat piece of board, or on a table where it can lie flat for several hours without being moved. I suggest a flat board because it will give support to the plaster-filled mold and therefore can be picked up and moved within a half-hour or so of pouring the plaster. Be sure that whatever surface you have chosen is level, or your casting will come out lopsided. You may want to place fairly heavy strips of straight wood along the edges of the mold, so that when the plaster is poured, the sides of the mold will be supported against the weight of the plaster, and will not sag.

When everything else is completely ready, mix your plaster. Be sure to use an old bowl that will not be ruined if it winds up with plaster stuck to it. I like to use a flexible plastic bowl, and a rubber spatula for mixing. Estimate how much mixed plaster it will take to fill the mold, and then measure that amount of water into your bowl. Next measure enough plaster to give yourself the consistency of mixed plaster you want to work with. (I find that the best proportions for most plasters I have worked with are 2 parts water to 3 parts plaster of Paris. This gives a thick enough consistency to work with, but does not set too quickly. Be careful; if you use too much plaster in too little water, it will set so fast that you won't even have time to get it out of the bowl. Before you do your casting in the good mold, you may want to experiment with smaller, makeshift molds to find the proportions that work best for you.)

Sift your plaster into the water, stirring constantly. When the mixture is smooth, pour it into the mold. Hold your spatula very close to the bottom of the mold and pour the plaster over it; this way the plaster will not hit the mold with much force, and there will be less chance of its either denting the mold or splashing out. The plaster should set for you within about thirty minutes, but it should not be removed from the mold *for at least eight hours.*

When the plaster is sufficiently dry, it may be taken out of the mold. If you are clever, you will be able to get the mold off without damaging it so that you can make more castings from it if you wish. However, each time you do a casting, the weight of the plaster makes the relief of the mold just a little lower, so that usually you can't do more than two or three good castings from even the best aluminum foil mold.

Now that it is out of the mold, you can finish your casting almost any way you like—gold paint was used on the sample in Figure 47. You may want to give it an antique look, or you may want to paint it so that it matches the original stone from which it was taken. The matter of what kind of finish to put on the casting is so personal, and depends so much on what background the finished piece is going to be set against, that I will leave it completely to your own imagination and creativity. The only thing to be careful of is that your casting is dry enough to handle before you start finishing it. Be patient, and give it plenty of time, or it will break when you handle it.

The casting may be hung in several ways. If it is relatively lightweight, and not too bulky, you can use epoxy glue to attach simple picture hangers to the back of it. If it is too heavy for this, then mount it on a wooden plaque, either by using epoxy to glue it on, or by drilling holes through it and attaching it with decorative wood screws. Once again, by using your imagination, you will be able to create all sorts of interesting and attractive effects.

FIGURE 47: *The finished plaster cast, painted gold. Later, it can be mounted for display.*

3. Some Rubbings by the Author

TOO OFTEN, it is assumed that the only "rubbables" to be found are kept deep within the confines of the early New England graveyard. And while I must admit that there are, indeed, many fine stones in New England, I must also admit that there are equally as many elsewhere. During my college years in Ohio, one of my braver friends and I spent many happy hours scouring the midwestern countryside for likely stones to rub; we would pour over Geodetic Survey maps and hike many a mile to find old and forgotten family graveyards left over from the days of the early settlers. The Ludwig Reed and Mary Horst rubbings are only two of the many that I collected then.

In the western states, most of the old gravestones are not stone, but rather are made of wood with the name and epitaph painted on rather than carved into the stone. As these "stones" weather, the unpainted surfaces erode faster than do the painted, creating slightly raised lettering which is just fine for rubbing. I have seen some beautiful rubbings taken from such markers—rubbings in which the letters have become clearly visible on a background of lovely wood grains.

In both Alaska and Hawaii, rubbing enthusiasts are seeking out petroglyphs, the primitive rock carvings of the ancient peoples of those states. In California, rubbings of gold-rush vintage are popular. And in New

York City, people have begun rubbing early manhole covers for a change of pace. I myself am hoping one day to be able to talk someone into letting me rub the intricate design-work on the inside of an early Wiebolt bank vault. Unfortunately, these are a little more strictly supervised than our early graveyards.

So you see, gravestone rubbing need not be limited to New England, and rubbing in general does not have to be limited to gravestones. Take a look at the rubbings that follow, and then go enjoy yourself doing some of your own.

FIGURE 48: *The urn-and-willow stone of Obadiah Osborn, Sudbury, Massachusetts, is more elaborate than most. As you can see, I have rubbed only part of the stone, and that took well over an hour.*

FIGURE 49: *No collection of rubbings would be complete without at least one stone of a man who, like Mehuman Hinsdell of Deerfield, Massachusetts, managed to get himself "Twice captivated by the Indian Salvages" and still lived to be sixty-three.*

FIGURE 50: *Here I've made a composite rubbing of Jabez Smith's stone (The Granary, Boston). Notice that in Figure 19 in the text only a half-circle surmounts the ship. I achieved a full circle simply by rubbing the stone as it is, then carefully removing the rubbing from the stone and turning it upside down, re-attaching it to the stone, and then filling in the rest of the circle.*

HERE LYES Y BODY OF
Mr JONATHAN SIMPSON
LATE OF BOSTON, WHO
DEPARTED THIS LIFE
NOVr 1st 1 7 3 3;
IN Y 54th YEAR OF
HIS AGE.

CHARLESTOWN doth claim his BIRTH
BOSTON his HABITATION,
SUDBURY hath his GRAVE
Where was his EXPIRATION.

FIGURE 51: *The life of Jonathan Simpson, Sudbury, Massachusetts, is neatly summed up in a verse.*

104

FIGURE 52: *The weathered marble stone of Mary Horst, near Smithville, Ohio, has a motif typical of many stones in Ohio.*

FIGURE 53: *Like many stones in and around Boston, the stone of Jonathan Poulter in Lexington, Massachusetts, includes many symbols—the death's-head, cross-bones, hourglass, soul effigies at the tops of columns of fruit or gourds—and two popular admonitions.*

106

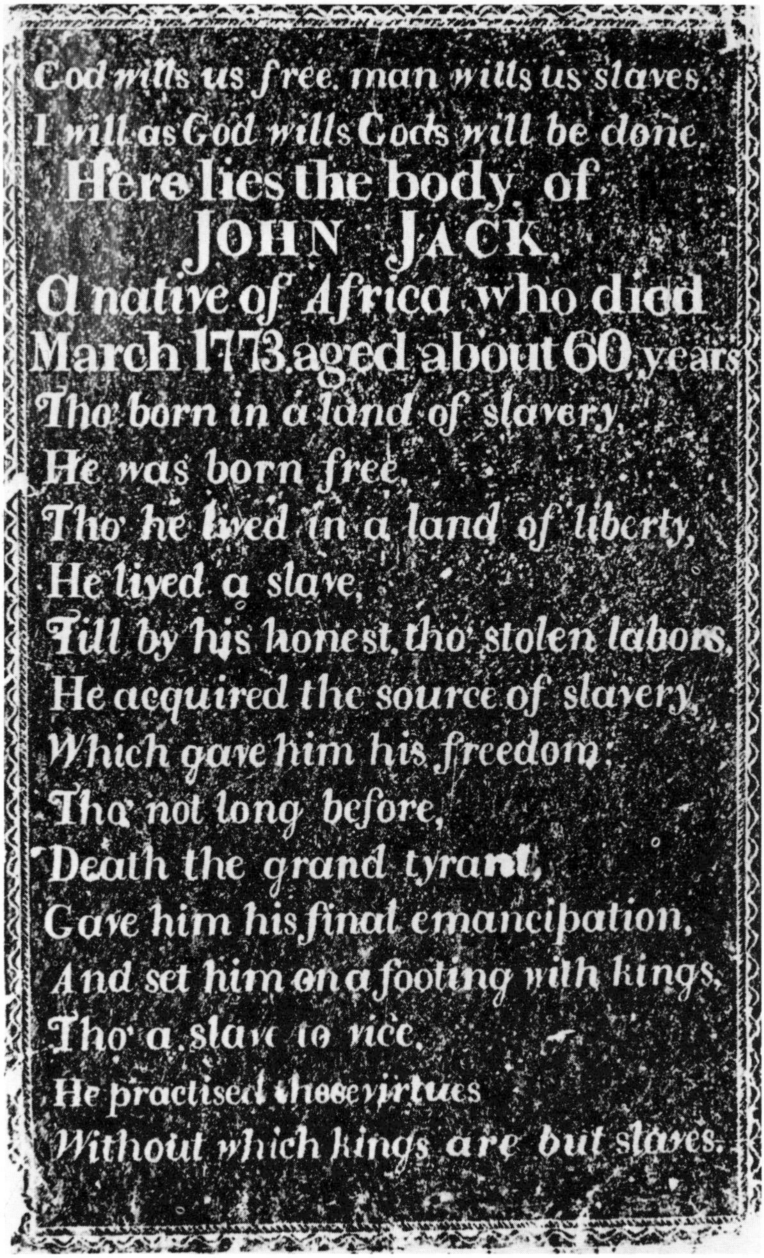

God wills us free. man wills us slaves.
I will as God wills Gods will be done.
Here lies the body of
JOHN   JACK.
A native of Africa who died
March 1773. aged about 60 years
Tho' born in a land of slavery,
He was born free.
Tho' he lived in a land of liberty,
He lived a slave,
Till by his honest, tho' stolen labors,
He acquired the source of slavery,
Which gave him his freedom:
Tho' not long before,
Death the grand tyrant,
Gave him his final emancipation,
And set him on a footing with kings,
Tho' a slave to vice,
He practised those virtues
Without which kings are but slaves.

FIGURE 54: *A simple stone with a beautiful verse (supposedly written by a Tory sympathizer), the stone of John Jack stands all the way at the back of the graveyard in Concord, Massachusetts. Legend has it that John Jack was the first slave in Concord and that after he bought his freedom he spent the rest of his days running a small store.*

In memory of
CAESAR

Here lies the best of slaves
Now turning into dust;
Caesar the Ethiopian craves
A place among the just.

His faithful soul has fled
To realms of heavenly light,
And by the blood that Jesus shed
Is changed from Black to White.

Jan. 15. he quitted the stage
in the 77ᵗʰ year of his age,
1780.

FIGURE 55: *We may laugh at the epitaph on Caesar's stone in North Attleboro, Massachusetts, but the man who wrote it was completely serious.*

FIGURE 56: *Mary Goose, who was buried near her daughter Susana in The Granary, Boston, may have been the legendary "Mother Goose."*

FIGURE 57: *Although Ludwig Reed's stone in Stoutsville, Ohio, contains little in terms of elaborate verse or motif, it is typical of stones that have weathered into a beauty of their own. Here we see a star-burst with its own trail of stardust falling over the handsomely carved German script.*

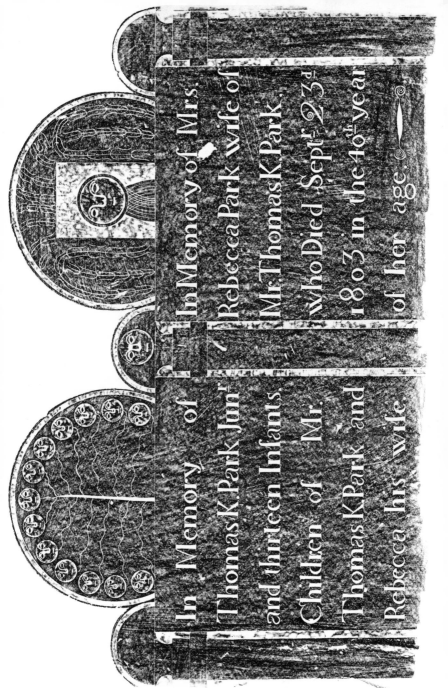

FIGURE 58: *This stone commemorating the Park family in Grafton, Vermont, was carved by the Wrights. Its motif is based on the tree of life, hung with thirteen little soul effigies.*

FIGURE 59 (above): *Also carved by the Wrights, the Lucinda Day stone in Chester, Vermont, shows a soul being carried heavenward in the belly of an eagle. Many authorities think that this motif was probably derived from a tavern sign of the day.*

FIGURE 60 (opposite): *The stone of John Kendall in Tyngsboro, Massachusetts, is both signed and dated: "Engraved by A. Webster. 1761."*

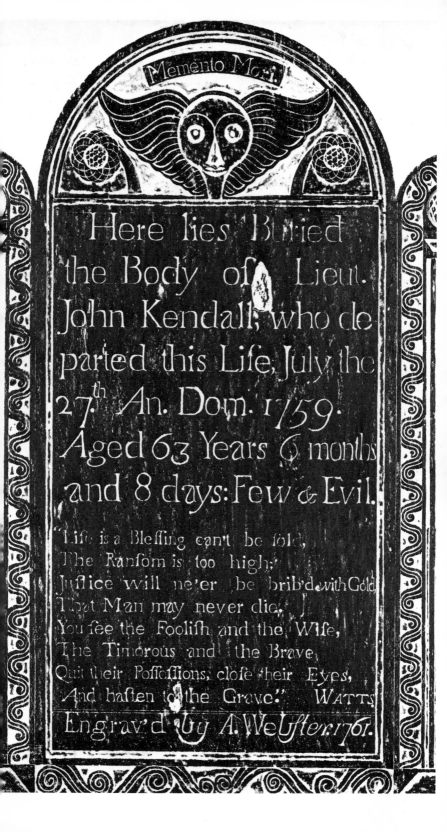

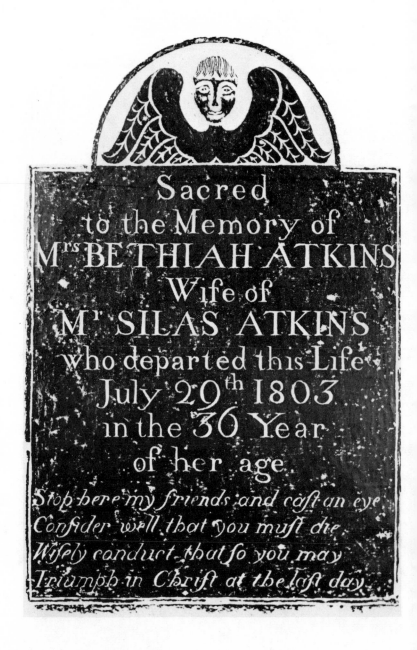

Sacred
to the Memory of
Mrs BETHIAH ATKINS
Wife of
Mr SILAS ATKINS
who departed this Life
July 29th 1803
in the 36 Year
of her age

Stop here my friends and cast an eye
Consider well that you must die
Wisely conduct that so you may
Triumph in Christ at the last day

FIGURE 61: *The inscription on the Bethiah Atkins stone on Cape Cod inspired the title for this book.*

114

⊷ BIBLIOGRAPHY AND
READING SUGGESTIONS ⧓

Besson, Frank L. *Epitaphs: a Guide to Old Burial Hill.* 1972, Oldstone Press, Marblehead, Mass.

Bodor, John. *Rubbings and Textures.* 1968, Rheinhold Book Corporation, New York.

Brown, Raymond Lamont. *A Book of Epitaphs.* 1969, Taplinger Publishing Company, New York.

Busby, Richard J. *Beginner's Guide to Brass Rubbing.* 1969, Pelham Books Ltd., London.

Clayton, Muriel. *Catalogue of Rubbings of Brasses and Incised Slabs.* Her Majesty's Stationery Office, London.

Forbes, Harriette M. *Gravestones of Early New England and The Men Who Made Them.* 1927, Houghton-Mifflin Publishers, Boston.

Gillon, Edmund V., Jr. *Early New England Gravestone Rubbings.* 1966, Dover Publications, New York.

Hall, Alonzo C. *Grave Humor.* 1961, Heritage Printers, Inc., Charlotte, North Carolina.

Kippax, John R. *Churchyard Literature.* Originally published 1877. Reissued 1969, Singing Tree Press, Book Tower.

Lindley, Kenneth. *Of Graves and Epitaphs.* 1965, Hutchinson & Company, Ltd., London.

Ludwig, Allan. *Graven Images (New England Stonecarving and its Symbols, 1650–1815).* 1966, Wesleyan University Press, Middletown, Conn.

Mann, Thomas C. and Greene, Janet. *Over Their Dead Bodies,* 1962, and *Sudden and Awful,* 1968, The Stephen Greene Press, Brattleboro, Vermont.

McGeer, William. *Reproducing Relief Surfaces (A Complete Handbook of Rubbing, Dabbing, Casting, and Daubing)*. 1972, Minuteman Press, Concord, Mass.

Wallace, Charles A. *Stories on Stone*. 1954, New York.

✌ INDEX ❧

Illustrated pages are indicated in bold face.

745
Jacobs, G.

Stranger stop and
cast an eye: a
guide to grave-
stones and gravestone
rubbing